LOVE
STREAMS

Great Quotations Publishing Company, Inc.

Compiled by: Marlene Rimler
Cover Design by: Bridgewater Design Consultants
Typeset and Design by: Caroline Solarski
and Julie Otlewis

Published by Great Quotations Publishing Company, Inc.
1967 Quincy Court
Glendale Heights, Illinois 60139

ISBN: 1-56245-078-6

Printed in U.S.A.

*Love is a stream running free
inside the heart of you . . .
inside the heart of me.*

— ♥ —

*There is nothing
half so sweet in life
as love's young dreams.*

— *Thomas Moore*

*Just as the wave
cannot exist for itself,
but must always participate
in the swell of the ocean,
so we can never experience life
by ourselves,
but must always share
the experience of life
that takes place all around us.*

— *Albert Schweitzer*

—❤—

*In order to create
there must be a dynamic force, and what
force is more potent than love?*

— *Igor Stravinsky*

Love is a candle in the darkness.
With its light
you will find your way.

— ❤ —

There are two tragedies in life.
One is to lose your heart's desire.
The other is to gain it.

— George Bernard Shaw

*R*isk the truth
with those you love
and give them the gift
you would want for yourself.

— ❤ —

*W*hen people have light
in themselves,
it will shine out from them.
Then we get to know each other
as we walk together in the darkness,
without needing to pass our hands
over each other's faces,
or to intrude
into each other's hearts.

— *Albert Schweitzer*

That best portion of a good man's life,
his little, nameless, unremembered acts
of kindness and of love.

— William Wordsworth

— ❤ —

We never live so intensely
as when we love strongly.
We never realize ourselves so vividly
as when we are in the full glow
of love for others.

— Walter Rauschenbusch

There is the kiss
of welcome and parting;
the long, lingering, loving, present one;
the stolen, or the mutual one;
the kiss of love, of joy, and of sorrow;
the seal of promise
and receipt of fulfillment.

—*Thomas C. Haliburton*

— ♥ —

We are all born for love.
It is the principle of existence,
and its only end.

—*Benjamin Disraeli*

*B*eauty —
the adjustment of all parts
proportionately
so that one cannot add
or subtract or change
without impairing the harmony
of the whole.

— *Leon Battista Alberti*

— ❤ —

*L*ove is . . .
Knowing that even when you are alone
you will never be lonely again.

*L*ove gives itself; it is not bought.

— *Henry Wadsworth Longfellow*

— ♥ —

*I*t has been written
that we are no greater than our dreams.
Dreams are the touchstones
of our characters.

— *Henry David Thoreau*

When a person that one loves
is in the world and alive and well . . .
then to miss them is only a new flavor,
a salt sharpness in experience.

— *Winifred Holtby*

— ♥ —

A place is nothing,
not even space,
unless at its heart a figure stands.

— *Amy Lowell*

*C*ompassion is an act of tolerance
where kindness and forgiveness reign.
When we make the compassionate choice,
we enhance the dignity
of each individual,
which is the very essence
of loving them.

— ❤ —

*T*o love someone
is to be the only one
to see a miracle invisible to others.

— *Francois Mauriac*

*L*ove consists of this,
that two solitudes protect and touch
and greet each other.

— *Rainer Maria Rilke*

— ❤ —

*N*o love, no friendship
can cross the path of our destiny
without leaving some mark on it forever.

— *Francois Mauriac*

*All our dreams can come true —
if we have the courage
to pursue them.*

— Walt Disney

— ♥ —

*Hold fast to dreams,
for if dreams die,
life is a broken winged bird
that cannot fly.*

— Langston Hughes

The one thing
we can never get enough of is love.
And the one thing
we never give enough of is love.

— *Henry Miller*

— ❤ —

*H*uman love . . .
It is that extra creation
that stands hurt and baffled
at the place of death . . .
Being human,
wanting children and sunlight
and breath
to go on, forever.

— *Christopher Leach*

Time flies,
suns rise and shadows fall.
Let time go by.
Love is forever.

— ♥ —

While faith
makes all things possible,
it is love
that makes all things easy.

The fountain of beauty is the heart,
and every generous thought
illustrates the walls of your chamber.

— *Francis Quarles*

———❤———

*C*reate the world you dream of
with every choice you make.

You will find
as you look back upon your life
that the moments
when you have really lived,
are the moments
when you have done things
in the spirit of love.

— *Henry Drummond*

— ❤ —

What will we hold tomorrow,
but the love we give today?

Love is the emblem of eternity,
it confounds all notion of time,
effaces all memory of a beginning,
all fear of an end.

— *Anna Louise De Stael*

———❤———

Love alone is capable
of uniting living beings
in such a way as to complete
and fulfill them,
for it alone takes them
and joins them
by what is deepest in themselves.

— *Pierre Teilhard De Chardin*

*B*e glad of life
because it gives you
the chance to love and to work
and to play
and to look up at the stars.

— *Henry Van Dyke*

— ❤ —

*H*appiness comes more from loving
than being loved.

—*J.E. Buchrose*

*L*ove is like the magic touch
of stars.

— *Walter Benton*

— ❤ —

*I*n real love
you want the other person's good.
In romantic love
you want the other person.

— *Margaret Anderson*

Love doesn't just sit there,
like a stone,
it has to be made,
like bread;
re-made all the time,
made new.

— *Ursula K. Le Guin*

— ❤ —

To love deeply in one direction
makes us more loving
in all others.

— *Anne-Sophie Swetchine*

Love one another,
but make no bond of love;
Let it rather be a moving sea
between the shores of your souls.
Fill each other's cup,
but drink not from one cup.
Give one another of your bread,
but eat not from the same loaf.
Sing and dance together
and be joyous,
but let each one of you be alone.

— *Kahlil Gibran*

— ♥ —

Love is the river of life
in this world.

— *Henry Ward Beecher*

The cure for all the ills and wrongs,
the cares, the sorrows,
and the crimes of humanity,
all lie in that one word "love".
It is the divine vitality
that everywhere produces
and restores life.

— *Lydia Maria Child*

— ♥ —

Happiness sneaks in through a door
you didn't know you left open.

— *John Barrymore*

If you have love in your life,
you can make up
for a great many things you lack.
If you don't have it,
no matter what else there is,
it's not enough.

— ❤ —

I love,
and the world is mine.

— *Florence Earle Coates*

*L*ove is something eternal.

—*Vincent van Gogh*

— ♥ —

*T*he supreme happiness of life
is the conviction
that we are loved.

—*Victor Hugo*

True hearts that share
one love, one life,
will always know true joy.

— *Jason Blake*

— ❤ —

There is the same difference
in a person
before and after he is in love,
as there is in an unlighted lamp
and one that is burning.
The lamp was there
and was a good lamp,
but now it is shedding light too
(and this is its real function).

— *Vincent van Gogh*

Living is one thing —
Loving is everything.

— ❤ —

Love:
To feel with one's whole self
the existence of another being.

— *Simone Weil*

The way to love anything
is to realize it might be lost.

— G.K. Chesterton

—❤—

Though time forgets,
still love remembers.

Look everywhere with your eyes;
but with your soul
never look at many things,
but at one.

— *V. V. Rozinov*

— ♥ —

Is it not by love alone
that we succeed in penetrating
the very essence of a being?

— *Igor Stravinsky*

*There is beauty all around
when there's love at home.*

— ❤ —

*The beginning of love
is to let those we love
be perfectly themselves,
and not to twist them
to fit our own image.
Otherwise we love only the reflection
of ourselves we find in them.*

— *Thomas Merton*

Love understands and gives
without restrictions.

— ❤ —

Love expects no reward.
Love knows no fear.
Love Divine gives —
does not demand.
Love thinks no evil;
inputs no motive.
To love is to share and serve.

— *Sivonada*

*T*he most powerful force on earth
is Love.

— ♥ —

*L*ove is an expression and assertion
of self-esteem,
a response to one's own values
in the person of another.

— Ayn Rand

*It is difficult to know
at what moment love begins;
it is less difficult to know
that it has begun.*

— *Longfellow*

— ❤ —

*Love is a butterfly,
which when pursued
is just beyond your grasp,
but if you will sit down quietly
it may alight upon you.*

— *Nathaniel Hawthorne*

To cheat oneself out of love
is the most terrible deception;
it is an eternal loss
for which there is not reparation,
either in time or in eternity.

— *Soren Kierkegaard*

—❤—

Life in abundance
comes only through great love.

— *Elbert Hubbard*

*The grand essentials
to happiness in this life
are something to do,
something to love
and something to hope for.*

— *Joseph Addison*

— ❤ —

*The way is not in the sky.
The way is in the heart.*

— *Gautama Buddha*

*L*ove is not a matter
of counting the years;
it's making the years count.

— *William Smith*

— ❤ —

*W*e can only learn to love
by loving.

— *Iris Murdoch*

We can do no great things —
only small things with great love.

— Mother Teresa

— ❤ —

Love is unselfish, understanding
and kind,
for it sees with its heart
and not with its mind.
Love is the answer
that everyone seeks —
Love is the language
that every heart speaks.
Love can't be bought,
it is priceless and free . . .
Love, like pure magic,
is a sweet mystery.

— Helen Steiner Rice

*W*hen you give love to someone,
you are banking it
for a later withdrawal.

— ❤ —

*W*here love is great,
the littlest doubts are fear;
when little fears grow great,
great love grows there.

— *Shaks*

*A*ny path is only a path,
and there is no affront,
to oneself or to others,
in dropping it
if that is what your heart tells you.

— *Carlos Castaneda*

— ❤ —

*L*ove is the sun
shining in us.

*Dreams are . . .
illustrations from the book
your soul is writing about you.*

— Marsha Norman

— ❤ —

*Love is everything.
It is the key to life,
and its influences
are those that move the world.*

— Ralph Waldo Trine

*I*s it not by love alone
that we succeed
in penetrating to the very essence
of a being?

— *Igor Stravinsky*

— ❤ —

*H*e has achieved success
who has lived well, laughed often,
and **loved much**.

*L*ove is the most important
ingredient of success.
Without it, your life echoes emptiness.
With it, your life vibrates warmth
and meaning.
Even in hardship, love shines through.
Therefore, search for love —
because if you don't have it,
you're not really living —
only breathing.

— ♥ —

*L*ove is a candle in the darkness.
With its light
you will find your way.

*O*ur visions begin with our desires.

— *Audre Lorde*

— ♥ —

*W*e are shaped and fashioned
by what we love.

— *Johann Wolfgang von Goethe*

Works, not words
are the proof of Love.

— ❤ —

Love doesn't grow on trees
like apples in Eden —
it's something you have to make.
And you must use
your imagination too . . .

— *Joyce Cary*

*Our desires must be like a slow
and stately ship,
sailing across endless oceans,
never in search of safe anchorage.
Then suddenly, unexpectedly,
it will find mooring for a moment.*

— *Etty Hillesum*

—❤—

*If I had never met him
I would have dreamed him into being.*

— *Anzia Yezierska*

*W*ho so loves believes the impossible.

— *Elizabeth Barrett Browning*

— ♥ —

I love you,
not because you're perfect,
but because you're so perfect for me.

*G*ive others the freedom
to be themselves.

— ❤ —

*S*ince love can be created,
there is no reason to be loveless.

*Y*ou can give without loving,
but you can never love without giving.

— ❤ —

*W*here there is love there is life . . .

— *Mahatma Gandhi*

*The love of your life
will love and accept you,
share your adventures,
and show you your folly.*

—❤—

*True love
doesn't have a happy ending;
true love
doesn't have an ending.*

Love understands love;
it needs no talk.

— *Francis Ridley Havergal*

— ❤ —

There is only one happiness in life,
to love and be loved.

— *George Sand*

This miracle
that happens every time
to those who really love:
the more they give,
the more they possess.

— *Rainer Maria Rilke*

— ❤ —

They gave each other a smile
with a future in it.

— *Ring Lardner*

*F*or as many times
as the waves embrace the shore,
is as many times
as I think of you.

— ♥ —

*L*ight tomorrow with today!

— *Elizabeth Barrett Browning*

*There is a magnet in your heart
that will attract true friends.
That magnet is unselfishness,
thinking of others first . . .
when you learn to live for others,
they will live for you.*

— *Paramahansa Yogananda*

—❤—

*Do you love me
because I'm beautiful,
or am I beautiful
because you love me?*

— *Oscar Hammerstein*

*The future belongs
to those who believe
in the beauty of their dreams.*

— *Eleanor Roosevelt*

—❤—

*One of the beautiful surprises
of middle age
is the discovery that mature love
is not only richer and deeper
but every bit as breathtaking
as it was in the beginning.*

*G*ive others a piece of your heart,
not a piece of your mind.

—♥—

*H*e who sows courtesy
reaps friendship,
and he who plants kindness
gathers love.

*To understand another
is one of life's richest blessings,
and to be understood by another
is perhaps love's sweetest
and most satisfying gift.*

— *Hemingway*

—♥—

*Absences are a good influence
in love
and keep it bright and delicate.*

— *Robert Louis Stevenson*

Love is
the immortal flow of energy
that nourishes, extends and preserves.
Its eternal goal is life.

— *Smiley Blanton*

— ❤ —

Two souls
with but a single thought.
Two hearts that beat as one.

— *Von Munch Bellinghausen*

*L*ove is the master key
that opens the gates
of happiness.

— *Oliver Wendell Holmes*

— ❤ —

*L*ove in your heart
wasn't put there to stay.
Love isn't love 'til you give it away.

*There is a land of the living
and a land of the dead
and the bridge is love,
the only survival,
the only meaning.*

— *Thornton Wilder*

—❤—

*Love looks not with the eyes,
but with the mind.*

— *William Shakespeare*

*R*ivers are roads which move,
and which carry us
whither we desire to go.

—*Blaise Pascal*

— ❤ —

*F*or true love is inexhaustible:
the more you give, the more you have.
And if you go to draw
at the true fountainhead,
the more water you draw,
the more abundant is its flow.

—*Antoine De Saint-Exupery*

*T*o fail to love
is not to exist at all.

— *Mark Van Doren*

— ♥ —

*T*ake away love
and our earth is a tomb.

— *Robert Browning*

*N*othing is impossible
to a willing heart.

— *John Heywood*

— ♥ —

*L*ove is the only gold.

— *Alfred Lord Tennyson*

*L*ove means the body,
the soul, the life, the entire being.
We feel love
as we feel the warmth of our blood,
we breathe love
as we breathe the air,
we hold it in ourselves
as we hold our thoughts.
Nothing more exists for us.

— *Guy De Maupassant*

— ❤ —

*L*ove is a chain of love
as nature is a chain of life.

— *Truman Capote*